# Boycott Blues

# Boycott Blues

## How Rosa Parks Inspired a Nation

### Andrea Davis Pinkney

### Illustrations by

### Brian Pinkney

Amistad

Greenwillow Books

An Imprint of HarperCollins Publishers

Boycott Blues: How Rosa Parks Inspired a Nation
Text copyright © 2008 by Andrea Davis Pinkney
Illustrations copyright © 2008 by Brian Pinkney
Amistad is an imprint of HarperCollins Publishers, Inc.
All rights reserved. Manufactured in China.
www.harpercollinschildrens.com

Colored inks on clay board were used to prepare the full-color art.
The text type is Adobe Caslon.

Library of Congress Cataloging-in-Publication Data
Pinkney, Andrea Davis.
Boycott blues: how Rosa Parks inspired a nation
by Andrea Davis Pinkney ; illustrated by Brian Pinkney.
p. cm.
"Greenwillow Books."
Summary: Illustrations and rhythmic text recall the December, 1955, bus boycott in
Montgomery, Alabama.
ISBN: 978-0-06-082118-0 (trade bdg.) ISBN: 978-0-06-082119-7 (lib. bdg.)
1. African Americans—Alabama—Montgomery—Juvenile fiction. [1. African Americans—
Fiction. 2. Civil rights demonstrations—Fiction. 3. Race relations—Fiction. 4. Montgomery
(Ala.)—History—20th century—Fiction.] I. Pinkney, J. Brian, ill. II. Title.
PZ7.P6333Boy 2008  [E]—dc22  2006038273

First Edition 10 9 8 7 6 5 4 3 2 1

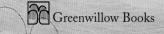 Greenwillow Books

To Dad —

A.D.P. & B.P.

Child, *child*.

You have not known weary till you have
walked in my shoes.
You have not known low-*down* till you
have sung my song.
You ever hear a dog wail?
You ever hear a hound moan?

Well, listen good. Because here it is.
Steady. Slow.
A story told with steps. With tired feet.
With tired *bones*.
I'm gonna tell the story with my guitar.
So you don't forget.
So you know how it goes.
Dog Tired, that's me.

This story begins with shoes.
This story is all for true.
This story walks. And walks. And walks.
To the blues.

It was December 1, 1955, when the blues came to call—the same day Jim Crow flew in waving his bony wings. Uh-*huh*. Bony wings and all, Jim Crow landed with a will. Yes he did, child. Yes he did.

Jim Crow was segregation. Laws that said black people and white people could not mix.

And on that day, it was Rosa Parks who got Jim Crow's *peck, peck, peck*, right up close.

Rosa Parks was a seamstress who worked at the Montgomery Fair department store. On that blue-as-blue evening, Rosa's workday ended like any other. She stepped onto the Cleveland Avenue bus and paid her dime to ride. The bus was packed tight. But Rosa spotted an empty seat one row behind the whites-only section. She sat down.

When the bus pulled up at the Empire Theater, several white people got on. All but one of them found seats. The last was left standing. That's when Jim Crow showed up—*struttin'*.

Whenever Jim Crow got to laying down the letter of the law, to stating the state of segregation, he did it with his *peck, peck, peck*. And on this day, Jim Crow's peck was a duet.

He was letting it fly with the bus driver, who, along with
Jim Crow, stood over Rosa and told her to give up her seat
to a white man who was still standing.
Even with that blue-black wing pressed at Rosa's nose.
Even with the bus driver's finger waving at Rosa. Even with
Jim Crow's *peck, peck, peck* sounding like rust on a
bedspring, Rosa stayed seated.
Twice the bus driver told Rosa to move. Twice she
looked at him without blinking, then turned her eye
to Jim Crow. All she said was no.
"You're breaking my law," Jim Crow crooned.
The bus driver said he'd call the police.
Rosa told him to go ahead.

The police arrested Rosa and took her to jail. Rosa's friend,
E.D. Nixon, raised money for Rosa's bail. He got her released
and told Rosa that if she were brave enough, she could stomp out
Jim Crow. She could break those bony wings. She could stop Jim Crow's
*peck, peck, peck.* She could help end segregation. Rosa agreed right away.
On December 5, 1955, the black people in town stopped
riding the city buses. They were protesting the treatment
Rosa had received.

That night, at the Holt Street Baptist Church, Martin Luther King Jr. spoke to the people of Montgomery.

Child, *child*. I have put my doggie tail in that church every Sunday. But I have never seen so many folks at Holt. People came from all over to hear the great Dr. King.

He said that we should "fight until justice runs down like . . . a mighty stream." And fight we did. We fought a quiet fight. No slingshots. No weapons. Not even spitballs. We fought with our feet.

We said if you *don't*, we *won't*. If you *don't* let us ride in any seat we wish, we *won't* ride at all. If you *don't* treat us fairly, we *won't* pay the fare. If we *don't* pay the fare, you *won't* have a bus business. And we *won't* let Jim Crow smack us back with his bony wings. Or slow us up with his *peck, peck, peck*.

Uh-*uh*. We *won't*.

And we stood by our word. Yes we did.

Child, *child*. We did.

That's when our feet took to the streets.
To the sidewalks. To the roads.
That's when the city buses rolled and rolled.
Nearly empty, they rolled.

That's when the boycott blues truly began—when we walked. With dogged feet. With dog-tired feet. With boycott feet. With boycott blues.

Ninety days passed. We kept on.

A hundred days gone. We stayed strong.

Walked in the rain, we did.

Walked day and night, we did.

Walked for our fight, we did.

Yes, we did.

Uh-*huh*, child, we did!

One hundred twenty days.
One-thirty. One-fifty.
Walked to work, we did.
Walked to school, we did.
Walked to church, we did.
Yes, we did, child. Yes. We did.

One hundred eighty days of walking.

One hundred degrees in the shade.

Sidewalks steaming.

Sweaty faces gleaming.

Hot dust rising off the roads.

And the buses rolled and rolled.

When the blues burned so blue-hot that they turned our beat to a deep blue shade of determination, we found a way out of no way. We found other modes to get to where we needed to go.

Soon, instead of only walking, we rode.
Rode with our friends, we did.
Rode with kind strangers, we did.

Rode past those empty buses, we did.

Uh-*huh*. We did. Yes, child. We did.

Didn't set foot on a bus, either. No, sir, we didn't.

Wouldn't pay our dime to ride, either. Uh-uh.

We still got to where we needed to go.

We still stood by Rosa Parks for saying no.

But Jim Crow, he was determined, too. He kept up
with his bony wings, and his *peck, peck, peck.*

Two hundred days later, we were still going.
Blues and all. We pressed *on*.

It wasn't all black folks boycotting, either. Some white
people came along for the ride, too—to show us support.
To help end Jim Crow.

Soon there were all kinds of people with keep-going feet.
With can't-stop-us feet. There were black folks *and* white folks
with the boycott blues.

And time walked on. And on.
Day two-twenty.
Day two-sixty-two.
Three hundred days of walking with
the boycott blues.

As strong as we were, some wanted to quit. And child, *child*,
I can't say I blamed them. After all, when you've been walking
from *De*-cember to *No*-vember, a bus begins to look like a sweet
temptation. Even *if* it means riding in the back. Even *if* Jim Crow
sits in your lap.

When I saw somebody start to go down that road, when I
heard somebody say, "What's the use? I'm paying my dime to
ride," I played my guitar as loud as I could to drown out
Jim Crow's *peck, peck, peck*. To stir up a rhythm worth
following. To somehow soften those boycott blues.
*Just a few more steps, and we're there.* I strummed
my message loud and clear.

Then came the miracle. The Supreme Court invited Jim Crow
in for a visit, and waved a gavel on his bony wings. The judge
in the courthouse said, "Jim, you're all wrong."
Right then, Jim Crow grew tired. His bony wings
started to ache. His *peck, peck, peck* began to lose its
point. Oh, child, that was a happy day!
On November 13, 1956, when the Supreme
Court struck down the segregation laws, the
bus drivers of Montgomery, Alabama,
were forced to say we *will*. We *will* let
black people sit wherever they want
on city buses. We will *not* practice
segregation any more.

And the black folks of Montgomery said *we* will. We *will* pay our dime. We *will* ride with pride. We *will* sit at the front of the bus and enjoy our view of justice.

On December 21, 1956, the law was official. Soon after, black people had a front-row seat, right behind the driver. So did Rosa Parks.

That was day three-eighty-two, when Jim Crow flew away. He had no more power in Montgomery.

It was the blues that got us through. It was the blues that helped our stride. Because blue is a so-fine color when it's painting the sky. Blue is the promise of possibility when it's coming on as the dawn. Blue is all beauty when it's flowing through a sea of hope.

Now segregation was a loser's croon.
And child, *child*, we rejoiced.
Our low-down tune changed to
a celebration song.

So, child, *child*, that's the end of my tale.

Now you know how it goes.

Now you see the power of won't-stop shoes.

Now you know the story of the boycott blues.


Time to hightail it home.

Bony wings, adieu.

*Peck, peck, peck,* later for you.

Bye-bye, boycott blues.

# Author's Note

When the Montgomery bus boycott began, the white residents of the city expected it to last no longer than a few days. Instead, the boycott served as a year-long movement that expressed the frustration many black people felt about the unfair treatment they had received.

On many occasions, white government officials tried to meet with black leaders in an effort to reach a compromise. Though several meetings occurred, there was no resolution. Montgomery business owners soon realized the boycott was not a short-term struggle. White merchants became worried for the welfare of their businesses, as black people no longer spent as much time or money in downtown establishments.

As time wore on, anti-boycotters tried to undermine the boycott. Black residents waiting for rides were sometimes arrested for hitchhiking. Insurance carriers made it difficult for black carpool drivers to get insurance policies.

False rumors about the boycott's end began to circulate. In January 1956 a local newspaper announced the boycott was over, saying a settlement had been reached between white government officials and black ministers.

More than forty thousand Montgomery residents participated in the boycott. While most of these were everyday people, their collective fortitude had a tremendous effect. Many believe the Montgomery bus boycott's greatest impact was that it sparked the nation's Civil Rights Movement and brought Martin Luther King Jr.'s vision of nonviolent resistance into America's consciousness.

The term "Jim Crow" is derived from a song performed in minstrel shows during the 1830s. Use of the term, which refers to the separation of races in public places, became popular in the 1880s, when racial segregation was made legal in many parts of the United States. For this story, I have taken the liberty of depicting Jim Crow as a menacing bird to give characterization to segregation's ugly reality.

Placing the Montgomery bus boycott against a backdrop of blues music pays tribute to a musical form that is rooted in the black tradition. Blues conveys the weariness of struggle, but at the same time can bring on a feeling of hope when truly expressed. Like a good cry, the blues are sharp and sweet at the same time. Even after the darkest night, things always seem brighter in the morning.

And who better to deliver this message than a dog-tired hound?

## For Further Exploring:

Altman, Susan. *Extraordinary African-Americans*. New York: Children's Press, 2001.

Carson, Clayborne, David J. Garrow, Gerald Gill, Vincent Harding, and Darlene Clark Hine, eds. *The Eyes on the Prize Civil Rights Reader*. New York: Viking Penguin, 1991.

*Eyes on the Prize: America's Civil Rights Movement*, DVD, directed by Henry Hampton (Blackside, Inc., 1987. PBS Video, 2006.).

Freedman, Russell. *Freedom Walkers: The Story of the Montgomery Bus Boycott*. New York: Holiday House, 2006.

Parks, Rosa, and James Haskins. *Rosa Parks: My Story*. New York: Dial Books, 1992.